P9-DUV-595

THE
QUIET MIND

Some further books of White Eagle's teaching:

THE
QUIET MIND

WHITE EAGLE

THE WHITE EAGLE PUBLISHING TRUST
LISS · HAMPSHIRE · ENGLAND

FIRST EDITION 1972
REPRINTED 1973, 1975, 1976,
1977, 1979, 1980, 1982, 1985, 1986, 1987, 1989, 1990
© COPYRIGHT, THE WHITE EAGLE PUBLISHING TRUST, 1972
ISBN 0-85487-009-1

Printed and bound in Great Britain by
William Clowes Limited, Beccles and London

CONTENTS

5

INTRODUCTION

The Quiet Mind comes in response to many requests for a collection of White Eagle's 'sayings' chosen to give guidance and help with the problems and experiences of everyday.

The title is from White Eagle's own words in Grace Cooke's book *Meditation*. 'The secret of strength lies in the quiet mind . . .'

A passage from the same book enumerates those qualities of soul revealed in the beautiful and perfect personality of the Master—qualities to which the disciple himself aspires on his own path towards mastership—and provides the framework for *The Quiet Mind*. For the sayings fall into groups arranged round each of these qualities in turn, to help us to face with courage and wisdom those trials of everyday, both great and small which come to test us, whether we ring true.

The passage in question reads:

'If you can think of yourself as being all that you know you should be: constant, gentle, loving and kind to every man, woman and child, and to every circumstance in life; kind and tolerant in your attitude towards all conditions on earth; above all, if you can conceive yourself as being completely calm in all conditions and circumstances, quiet and yet strong—strong to aid your weaker brethren, strong to speak the right word, to take the right action, and so become a tower of strength and light; if you can see yourself facing injustice and unkindness with a serene spirit, knowing that all things work out in time for good, and that justice is always eventually triumphant; if you have patience to await the process of the outworking of the will of God: if you can picture becoming like this, you will know something of mastership ...'

White Eagle speaks, not from a remote height, but as one who himself trod this way when on earth, through many, many lives. He speaks with authority, but with real and tender love and understanding; often with humour, always constructively, never critically.

If we can follow where he leads, each one of us can at least find strength and comfort in tribulation. At most, we shall find perfect happiness.

Let us never forget however that we do not walk alone, for, as White Eagle says, 'If the veil could be drawn aside, you would indeed feel happy and thankful to know that by the power and through the will of God, the spiritual brothers come close to help you on your upward climb. Try to feel the comfort of their warm handclasp—their hand upon your shoulder, their understanding. Your spiritual teacher and guide knows your every aspiration, every difficulty that you endure. Your guide knows your innermost need, and will comfort you and lead you into green pastures and beside still waters. By your love, by your belief in God's love, your belief in love itself, you can create the bridge across which we come to you.'

'Think of your Master as being very natural, very loving and simple. The more simple you are yourself the nearer you will be to realisation of his nature. He smiles upon you, and often his eyes twinkle with tender humour. When you think of him, remember the twinkling eyes, the tender humour and the wise understanding!'

'All God seeks from you, His child, is the devotion of your heart; He wants your heart for God, your heart for all that is good. For God is love, and he that loveth knoweth God and doeth what God wills; to him all things are possible. Have patience and keep on working for God.'

THE MASTER SOUL IS CONSTANT

In the mind of God dwells the picture of the perfect man, His Son, Christ—you! To God you are not the weak and erring child of earth; God holds you ever in His thought as the perfect form, the Christ-man, created in His own image.

HELP FROM ABOVE

If you will be steadfast on the path to which your feet have been guided, you will find the treasure of life, a never-ending stream of help and healing and happiness. We, your brothers and guides, are on the road by your side. Not one of you stands alone. You have only to ask in simple trust, and you shall receive; whatever your need, it shall be supplied.

ACTIVITY IN GOD

To love is to live in God. Loving is activity in God, so that every thought and action is in God—not in the world. When a man loves he no longer responds to the vibrations of destruction and death, but to those of the more abundant life.

FOCUS HEART AND MIND ON GOD

The one sustenance, the great sustaining power all mankind can receive, is strength from God. If you are sick in body, weary in mind, despondent and hopeless, turn your thoughts away from yourself. Turn your thoughts and your prayers and your praise to God; focus your whole heart and mind upon God. Never waver, never falter, hold fast to belief in the Great White Spirit; and in God's light you will find that every need of your life will be met.

RING TRUE

Be true. This is the essence of the spiritual life. The note of the spirit is sounded on the higher planes, and the knocks you receive in everyday life are to test you, whether you can ring true. To ring true you must always sound the note of God, or good, which is within you.

KEEP ON KEEPING ON

How often have we said, 'Keep on keeping on.' This means constantly pulling yourself up to the mark; it means a constant contact with your higher self, a putting aside of the claims of the lower self and a continual joyous giving, giving, giving to God, to mankind.

TRUE VALUES

You are spirit first and body last. Let your spirit so shine before men that they may see their Christ in you.

YOUR TRUE SELF

The first and greatest claim upon you is the claim of God, or of your spirit; or, in other words, your highest self. Your true self is a shining spirit. You must be true to that shining spirit above all things. Let nothing draw you aside from your soul's pursuit of truth and light and eternal love.

THE WAY TO PRAY

The way to pray is to put yourself into complete attunement with the spirit of love. Be in it, live in it. Think not of yourself and of your earthly need, but of God. Of yourself you are nothing: but when you dwell in the centre of the Star, or that heavenly Light, you become great because you are then consciously with God and God is with you; and all things work together for good when you are with good or with God.

TESTS AND DISAPPOINTMENTS

Every soul has to withstand great pressure and to be well tested. Supposing the Master called upon you to do an important piece of work which was going to involve many souls; and supposing you had not been tested and proved? It is possible that you would break down under the stress of the work. We are telling you this in order to help you in your endeavours to follow the path of light, with all its testings and disappointments.

Such a glorious opportunity stretches before each one of you. The trivialities of every day, the disappointments and the petty annoyances and the hurts which you allow yourselves to receive from daily life, are all very small; but you yourselves allow them to seem very big. Let them recede, concentrate your whole being upon the love of God. Be His child! Surrender your self-will to the divine Will.

THE LIFE-GIVER

Children, there is no death, and there need be no weariness of the flesh. There is no weariness when the soul has entered into the full glory of the Sun, the Almighty One. May all tiredness and weariness be dispelled by the inflowing Life-giver, the Sun!

Don't bow down to mammon, and all the material difficulties and problems of the world. If instead you will turn to worship God with all your heart and soul and mind, all the cares of mortal life will be dissolved, because they will have no part in you, no abiding place in your heart. The Christ in you can deal in a masterly way with these perplexities.

SECURITY

Walk each day in childlike faith, with your hand clasped in the hand of your Master. That hand is the hand of truth, it is security, it will never fail you. Earthly men may fail you but never your Master. And in seeking your Master, let this thought help you, that you will find him, you will see him and hear his voice speaking to you, when you have learnt to overcome the 'not-self,' or the lower self, and to think always and speak as your higher self commands.

KEEP YOUR CONTACT

Whenever you are tired or weary, seek the Presence of the Golden One, and draw into your soul His love, His gentle beauty, His refreshment. If you can keep your certain, sure contact with God, nothing can go wrong in your life. You have no need to worry about decisions whether to do this, that or the other. Your decisions will be made for you, but you must be awakened to the spirit, quickened in spirit, so that you will instantly respond to the gentle guidance of the almighty Presence within you.

'Watch and pray' are not idle words. Follow the light as it breaks in your own heart; obey the voice of your inner spirit, do those things which you know are right.

DWELL OFTEN ON THOUGHTS OF GOD

The power which comes when the heart is set upon God can reverse negative to positive, darkness to light; the inflowing of the light will produce perfect health because it will produce harmony.

LOVE IS LIGHT, AND LIGHT IS LIFE

Never concentrate on disease or darkness; concentrate on harmony, light. Centre your whole thought upon the spirit of the Lord Christ, the gentle Master, then the weariness of the flesh will fall away from you because by your own inner effort you are transmuting those dark atoms into light. If you could live always in the Light you would need no healing from outside—the Light itself would heal you.

THE PRESENCE OF CHRIST

At all times keep in your heart the thought of the presence of Christ; remember His ever-peacefulness and calm amidst the turmoil of worldliness. You who are His disciple must ever seek to find the place of quietude and sweetness in the midst of the crowd. It is easy in solitude to be close to Him, but you must learn to become aware of your Master, despite the crowding of the multitude.

... IS GENTLE, LOVING, KIND

OVERCOME EGOTISM

One of the first lessons or aspirations of a brother, one of the points of brotherhood, is to overcome egotism; then the flowers of the spirit bloom and you have your saint. A saint is human, is understanding; a saint is able to enter into all the feelings, the joys and the sorrows of another. A saint is all love.

THE BROTHERHOOD LOVE YOU

Ministers of God are by your side; no single detail in your life, not a thought or an action, escapes them. But they judge not, they only love, with deep compassion and wide understanding. Remember this and pray that a love such as theirs will fill your heart so that you look upon all men with the same gentle loving kindness as the Brethren of the Light regard you.

NO COMPROMISE

If the action of another irritates you and you chafe under a sense of injustice, do not try to attack, even in your thoughts, the one who appears to have offended. Have you not given yourself to the Master of Love? There can be no compromise; your way is clearly shown. It is the way of love, gentleness, peace.

THE HEALING POWER OF LOVE

The emotion of real love is Light, and if we think of the suffering in the world with compassion, as we imagine Christ thought of it, we can send forth a great Light which will find a resting place in the heart of the weary and the sad and the sick, and will in time create a new life, a new body.

WHEN YOU ARE CONFUSED

When you come up against a difficulty and there is confusion and misunderstanding, go into your innermost sanctuary. Seek the presence of the gentle Christ, and ask what He would do in the circumstances in which you are placed.

LAY DOWN YOUR PROBLEM

Cast your burden upon the Lord. In other words, let go, surrender, lay down your problems. Do not try to unravel the knot, which gets tighter and tighter as you pull at it. Lay it down. Concentrate all your heart upon that gentle, loving personality, the Lord Jesus Christ, and all knots will be unloosed, all problems solved.

As you surrender your will to God, and have faith and confidence in the love of God, so will that love be continually demonstrated to you and will work out in your lives. If you live in accordance with spiritual law you will harm no man and no man can harm you.

WISE LOVE

The Master takes notice of your every effort to perfect the nature of love. . . . He understands your failures and your triumphs, and continues to pour His love upon you. If He who is so beautiful, so great in spirit, can continue to love you, in spite of all, is it so hard for you to give your little love to your brother man, and all living things? But there is much to learn in the lesson of brotherhood; bear in mind that love divorced from wisdom is no longer love. You must learn to distinguish between true, impartial and compassionate love, and emotionalism, which will sweep you off your feet and destroy love. To love is to give the highest and truest within you to your brother; to love is to give the Light from your own soul, the White Light of Christ. This is love.

APPLY LOVE TO YOUR PROBLEM

Love is the great solvent of all difficulties, all problems, all misunderstandings. Apply love, by your inner attitude towards any human problem. Put aside the reasoning mind. Let divine love operate in you. Give from your inner self God's love, and you will be surprised to find that every problem will be solved; every knot loosened.

BE COMFORTED, BE AT PEACE

Be comforted. Be comforted, dear ones; there is eternal life for all souls who love God, Who is love; and where there is love there can be no separation. Your loved one is by your side. Death cannot separate you. Be comforted and at peace.

WHEN YOU ARE AT VARIANCE . . .

When you come up against personal hurts try to attune yourself to the heights, to the Form of the Golden One enthroned in the blazing Sun, and as you hold that vision, think of the one with whom you are at variance and a shaft of Light will go to him and there will be a change in the position and all will go smoothly. Thus are crooked places made straight.

THE MASTER'S WAY

The wise man does not argue, he remains silent and goes quietly on his path, concerned only with learning to follow in the footsteps of his Master.

Understand that you yourselves must work in your everyday life; it is your reactions to daily events and to the conditions of life that really bring about attunement, achievement. It is no good listening to White Eagle or to any other teacher unless you yourself work for self-mastery. The beginning of this work is your awareness of the still small voice within, of that gradually increasing Light in you which causes you to react as a gentle brother to all the conditions and all the circumstances of life.

LOVE IS AN INWARD BEAUTY

To love is to give the Christ spirit within, without any thought of return. You are all so apt to feel that you must have a return for your love, but the soul has to learn to *give love*. Love is an inward beauty which flows from the heart, from the life.

27

Let love rule. There is nothing to fear except fear. Fear is man's enemy and the last to be overthrown. Have no fear. Resign all to the wisdom and the love embodied in divine law. Do your best. Be true and sincere and loving in your human relationships. Let love rule your heart and life.

BE GENTLE WITH YOURSELF

Jesus said: 'Thou shalt love thy neighbour *as thyself.*' This does not mean selfishness; it means kindliness to yourself because you are God's child. Do not give yourself more attention than you need, but take care of yourself and do not continually slay the God within you. Give opportunities in your daily life for the Christ within to manifest itself. This is what we mean by loving yourself, and this is what Jesus meant when he said: 'Thou shalt love thy neighbour *as thyself.*' Love peace of

28

mind, love doing the right thing, love living according to divine law.

RELEASE COMES WITH FORGIVENESS

To forgive is often difficult, my children; but with forgiveness release comes to the spirit; the soul that has been in bondage and perhaps stretched upon the cross of suffering no longer suffers.

In the degree that you respond to love and beauty, so you are increasing beauty on earth; and by the same token decreasing that which lies on the other side of the scale—the darkness and ignorance and bitterness and selfishness of humanity.

THE WAY OF THE DISCIPLE

And how, you ask, are we to walk the spiritual path? We answer: Say little; love much; give all; judge no man; aspire to all that is pure and good—and keep on keeping on.

. . . IS TOLERANT

LOVING MEANS SEEING GOOD

You must learn so to act, so to live each day, that you are naturally, at all times, a being of love. Love is not sentimentality. Love is seeing good, seeing God, recognising the divine law of cause and effect working throughout all life. To love is to be tolerant towards all men, towards all the happenings of daily life; to be patient, thoughtful, kind and meek. All these qualities are contained in the one word—love.

LOOK BELOW THE SURFACE

Do not judge by what you see on the surface, but develop an inner vision and insight into spiritual cause and effect. Then you will know that you can judge no man.

We shall do well to remember how much we ourselves need forgiveness, and to learn to forgive freely, judging no man. We know not any soul; but it is our duty, our surpassing joy, to search ever for the spark of the divine in all men.

MAGIC THAT HEALS

There is always something beautiful to be found if you will look for it. Concentrate on beauty rather than on the reverse. This positive, loving attitude towards life and people is all part of the divine magic which we are endeavouring to reveal to you. It is helping you to perceive the divine Presence, helping you to put into operation the divine magic which heals.

Withhold judgment and criticism. The human way is to judge in haste the actions of others, but the divine way is to remain quiet and loving. You are divine as well as human and are here on earth, to learn to manifest divinity.

THE ELDER BRETHREN DO NOT JUDGE

The Elder Brethren labour ceaselessly for you and for all men. They do not get angry nor do they judge their younger brethren, because they know God's laws, God's plan for the unfoldment of the God within man. The young in soul are quick to pass judgment on others; but the Elder Brethren are patient; they do not expect too much.

BE THANKFUL FOR YOUR KARMA

Do not criticise your brothers, for this brings about disintegration in your own being, in your own life. Instead, look in love and thankfulness on those with whom your karma has brought you into association.

THE LIFE THAT MAKES ALL THINGS NEW

God-in-man makes all things new. When man realises the Christ Spirit within, everything changes for him. For then he begins to see beauty instead of ugliness, love instead of hate; to realise health instead of sickness. The world becomes fresh and new, as when after rain you can look out on an earth washed clean, and shining with the sunlight.

THE SLEEPING PRINCESS

Often you see only the rough practical exterior of a man or woman. If only you could cut away the thorns, you would find a gentle and beautiful nature beneath, sleeping. Strive always to find the princess hidden behind all prickly growths. We all possess the Light within; we all have that higher, that *princess* self. We should therefore deal with each other lovingly, always seeking the best, and encouraging beauty in every possible way.

HAPPINESS BEYOND YOUR DREAMS

You can purify your own physical atoms by right thinking, right speech, right action, right living, judging no man; then, imperceptibly, will come a raising of your consciousness, a happiness of which you have not dreamed, and a gracious and gentle power will grow within you which will make all crooked places straight, and which will open your prison doors—even as the angel touched the door of Peter's prison and set him free.

'Forgive us our trespasses as we forgive those who trespass against us.' The words come to you in love, and are to help you when you are in trouble and difficulty. When emotions threaten to overwhelm you, just forgive, and all shall be forgiven, and God will bless you, my child.

FORGIVENESS

Have you ever thought what forgiveness means? You, your own self, your own personality, needs your forgiveness. Your spirit is divine, but until you have overcome, your personality remains human and needs the forgiveness of your spirit. As you forgive, as your spirit forgives your personality, so also you will learn to forgive your brother man for all his seeming errors. If you will train yourself to think in terms of love and forgiveness every moment of your life, a most beautiful healing will take place in you.

IN THE PRESENCE OF THE MASTER

In the presence of the Master anger and resentment dissolve; you are filled with peace, overcome with adoration and love. Your consciousness is instantly raised above the pulls and antagonisms of the earthly plane.

RESPECT YOUR BROTHER

The true Light is a gentle love which, rising in you, causes you to look on the world with understanding and compassion and *respect*. When you respect the soul of your brother man you respect his life in every way. This gentle spirit, this respect one for another, must come. For this is the generation of the one true Light, and this true Light is that of love.

If you are delayed, if your work does not seem to be developing as you hoped, do not be despondent or disheartened, but be thankful that you are being trained for greater initiation. No great or good work is ever accomplished without patient preparation. Every detail of the soul's work must be perfectly done. So be patient in your work, patient with all the happenings of your daily life, and especially be patient with your fellows.

... IS CALM, QUIET AND STEADY

I AM WITH YOU

Whatever ordeal lies before you, remember the Christ Presence, for it will never leave you; it brings peace and courage. *Lo! I am with you always.*

GOD WILL NOT FAIL YOU

When in doubt, do nothing. Be still, have patience and wait. Learn to be still, my children, to be calm and still and wait for God; God will not fail you.

BENEATH THE CLAMOUR OF THE WORLD

You long for peace. You think of peace as being goodwill towards each other, goodwill among the nations, the laying down of arms. But peace is far more than this, it can only be understood and realised within your heart. It lies beneath all the turmoil and noise and clamour of the world, beneath feeling, beneath thought. It is found in the deep, deep silence and stillness of the soul. It is spirit: it is God.

THE CENTRE OF PEACE

Pray, 'Lead me, Heavenly Father, show me the way.' But it is no good appearing calm outwardly while remaining a seething volcano inwardly. You must develop inner calm. Daily seek for that still centre within your soul which is the abiding place of the Christ spirit.

THE MASTER OF YOUR LODGE

You become over-driven and disturbed by little things, petty things. This you must not do. Pray to be the master in the lodge of your own being. Learn to rule your lodge with love and truth, wisdom and beauty.

SEEK THE GREATER, LET THE LESSER GO

We would remind you very tenderly that you pay too much attention to earthly values. We do not mean that you should neglect your earthly duties, but we suggest that you should get a clearer understanding of the relative values of spiritual and earthly things; for so much that you consider necessary and important to you is not important. If you will seek always the stillness, the peaceful spirit of the Lord Christ, you will find that through this you open the windows of your soul, and the light of the Christ Spirit will flood your soul and life; and that which seemed to you to be a trouble and an anxiety will be absorbed into the light.

MY PEACE I GIVE UNTO YOU

The Master is tender and loving; he knows your need, he understands your difficulties and disappointments and says, 'Come, brother, come above the mists, come unto me, and I will give you that inner peace for which you long . . .'

WHERE PEACE ABIDES

Peace and healing lie within the heart of God. Live in the heart of God . . . there is no fear there.

RELAX THOSE TENSED NERVES . . .

Be at peace, beloved child; relax those tensed nerves . . . relax just for five minutes, and concentrate on the Presence of the Lord Christ. Imagine you can see him in his golden glory. Feel his love flowing to you. Trust him, for good, and only good is coming to you; but do not stop its coming by being worried and anxious.

POISE

The brethren of the Great White Lodge are happy because they are at peace, undisturbed by dark happenings. You will say, 'Is it right to be undisturbed by the dark things?' Yes, my child, because by maintaining inner peace and letting the Light burn steadily within you, you are doing far more good than if you get excited and argumentative about disagreeable conditions. Keep your poise; be steady on your path.

GOD KNOWS YOUR NEED

God knows every need of your body, your soul and your spirit. Learn to be calm and still, and do your best, with love in your heart. If you do your best, God will do the rest. Now trust in your best, and in God.

WORK QUIETLY

The answer to your own individual problem and heartache is to surrender all to God. Be still within, be calm. Do not try to overdrive your life. Be calm, do your work quietly; live as the flowers live, opening your heart to the sunlight of God's love.

WASTE NOT

Learn to conserve energy and to control the emotional and mental expenditure and wastage continually taking place in everyday life. A Master has learned the supreme lesson of the conservation of energy; he will never waste his energy, the vital force, the God-life. He trains himself to remain calm and tranquil in spite of the storms of life.

GOD NEVER HURRIES

Spiritual power moulds physical and material conditions, but spiritual power is never in a hurry. You want things to happen immediately, but God never hurries. There is all eternity in which to work and live and be joyful!

STILLING THE STORM

It is easy to be stirred and emotionally upset by contact with inharmonious conditions, but as the Christ Light within grows stronger it teaches the neophyte to control passion and emotion, to keep it stilled and in its right place, so that emotion can be used for spiritual service but is not allowed to storm through the soul upsetting and shattering it.

ETERNITY IS NOW

Learn that eternity is now, the future is now. There is no past or present or future as separate periods of time—all is within the soul's embrace now. It is your reaction to the *now* which is your future. Never look into the future and anticipate this, that, or the other, for to do so is to live in fear. Live today with God, and your future can hold nothing but joy.

LET NOTHING DISTURB THEE

In your daily life you can, by an effort of the Will of God within you, instantly attain, under any conditions, tranquillity of mind. Whatever the conditions, you can still the storm, and know tranquillity. You long to become aware of a life which is free, which is holy, happy, healthy and joyous, in which you can render service and see the Land of Light. We give you pointers . . . First, tranquillity of spirit. Let nothing disturb you. . . . When you allow things to disturb you, all the fine threads of colour and light attached to your soul from the Source of your life become tangled and jangled —in very truth you cross the wires. Then you wonder why things are so difficult. Don't cross the wires. Keep your line of contact clear. Be tranquil and serene. A Master is never perturbed.

LIVE IN GOD, IN GOD'S TIME

Live tranquilly in God, in God's time. Every morning on waking and every night before you sleep, send out a thought to the Great White Spirit, that is all. Just feel that He is in your heart and that you are the son-daughter of that living power; that whatever your need the Great White Spirit knows it.

MAN IS DIVINE

In the spheres of light, men are tranquil, with shining, God-like faces. Every piece of work is executed perfectly, and the effort of all is applied to further the happiness of the community. Always, in your inner selves and in your quiet moments, you can rise into this perfect life, and receive from those who dwell there the inspiration to live likewise on earth. Don't make the excuse that man is only human. With all the force of the truth that is in us, we say, we know, that man is divine.

YOUR CHRIST-SELF

Every day on awaking and many times during the day, particularly when you are being overwhelmed and harassed by the affairs of the physical life, pause and remember that it is the little self, the human personality which is being tried, and then understand that above you in the invisible realms is that greater self, the Christ-self. Look into that form of glorious colour, that radiant life, and you will feel infinite power flowing into your personality. You will be conscious, above your personality, of a self which is limitless, which is living in God.

47

DAILY LINK YOURSELF TO GOD

Cultivate inner calm, daily linking yourself to God in prayer and meditation, always giving Light from your spirit—never depression, only Light; and walking patiently and humbly on your path. You will then be recipients of the unfailing power of God, and reflectors of divine love.

ONE THING AT A TIME

When your tasks seem a little heavy and overwhelming remember just to do one thing at a time quietly, and leave the rest because the rest is not your job. What you cannot get through you must hand back to God, and He will work it out for you.

THE INFINITE AND ETERNAL GARDEN

Around you, or a little above you, maybe, is a beautiful garden, the infinite and eternal

Garden of the Spirit; from this state of life, with its beauty and peace, and the love of its inhabitants, we draw close to you in your physical life to help you. We come to raise you above the limitations of pain and grief, into that true home, that heavenly life from which you have all come, and towards which you are all journeying.

SEEK FIRST THE KINGDOM

Man has to learn to seek first the kingdom of heaven, the place of stillness and quiet at the highest level of which he is capable, and then the heavenly influences can pour into him, re-create him and use him for the salvation of mankind.

...IS STRONG TO SERVE

TO HEAL THE WHOLE WORLD

Behind you is a Power beyond your comprehension; God only waits for His children to be willing to be a channel; He only waits for you to serve, knowing that you are nothing. May the channel open wide and the light flood through! By your mental direction it can go forth to heal the nations, to heal the whole world.

THE MASTER'S SERVICE

You may be used at any moment for the Master's service, but because the call to service is not always what you were expecting, sometimes you do not realise that you have been called and chosen for the Master's work. Make ready in your hearts, for you know not the day nor the hour when the Master will come.

BE UNTIRING

Be untiring in your work, but depend not on your own strength. That would bring you limitation. Look to the Great White Spirit for all your needs and for the release of that inner strength. Be undaunted, be untiring, but depend not on yourself. Look to the infinite love and glory of the Son, Christ.

KEEP THE LIGHT BURNING

Keep the Light burning. There is nothing more important than to keep the Christ Light burning within. Only this will give you the power that you need to do those little acts of service that the Master asks of you.

As you work with courage and patience in your particular corner, so will you be rewarded by an ever-increasing consciousness of the companionship and the very real help in your material lives, given to you by your invisible brethren.

WHATSOEVER THY HAND . . .

It does not matter what your work is on the earth. What does matter is that you should do your work with all your heart and with all your strength and with all your mind. Pray also for wisdom that you may work in the right way, and for courage that you may not become faint-hearted on your path.

THE GOOD, THE TRUE, THE BEAUTIFUL

We beg you to hold fast to the good, the true and the beautiful, to be positively good in your outlook upon life, and positively to attune your minds and your souls to the influence of the messengers from other worlds. They are looking to you, to respond and to believe and to become channels for a continual outflowing of the Christ Spirit to stimulate and beautify all life.

I, IF I BE LIFTED UP . . .

If you endeavour to raise the Christ within you, you help to raise all mankind. You cannot make one effort towards heaven without the whole of the world, even the very earth itself, being the better for it. See the responsibility that lies with you, brethren! What a glorious opportunity is yours! Don't allow the darkness of earth to deny you your birthright of freedom and happiness, of service and worship. Peace be with you; peace, and a great joy.

LOOK INTO THE LIGHT

Your personal contribution towards the great plan for the evolution of man is to dwell continually upon the love of God; to look always into the light and so train yourself to recognise God's goodness working through everyone else.

THE SON IS BORN IN YOU

You long to do something to help others. We tell you that the greatest work of all is to develop the Christ Light within your soul. For the Son is born in you, in all humanity; and your special work, and ours, is to learn how to project that light into the darkness of ignorance on earth.

ACCEPT THE TASK

Each one of you has been called. Every individual soul has his own work to do. None can do the work of another. Each must do his own work. Therefore, we say, accept it, my child: accept the task laid before you and pray to the Great White Spirit that you may not fail.

HELP FROM ABOVE

You will receive help as you ask, not with your mind, but in the depths of your being, quietly. Pray to the God within you for help, and you need have no fear at all about your power to accomplish your given work.

FEET ON EARTH, HEAD IN HEAVEN

Keep your feet on the earth but lift your face towards the heavens, for the Light which floods into you from on high will steady your feet and guide them in the right path. Have confidence in this divine Light. Surrender with a tranquil mind and a heart full of love to this infinite Wisdom.

NEVER FORCE THE ISSUE

Never try to force the door and to go into any condition by force; just wait and you will conserve all the power which will be necessary for you to accomplish your work at the given time.

It may comfort you to know that every one of you who undergoes some experience involving pain and anguish, and which might be described as a crucifixion, is doing something for the whole world; for anyone who meets such testings of the soul in the same resolute and tranquil spirit (in however small degree), as did the Master Jesus, is helping to quicken the vibrations of the whole earth.

WHEN LOVE POSSESSES YOUR HEART

To serve adequately, the soul must make sacrifices. There must be sacrifice of desire and of self. Your Master demonstrated this, even to sacrifice of life itself. There is no true service without sacrifice. You may shrink from it, brothers, but you cannot alter the law of life. But, when love possesses your heart, all service, all giving, brings such joy that there is no sacrifice.

Whatever your occupation while in your physical body, remember it is a form of service. However humble or even humdrum your work may be to you, it is *your* special appointment, and through your work on earth you can make your contribution to the happiness of all. Work hand in hand with God, and be thankful for every opportunity to serve which is laid before you.

THE GREATEST SERVICE

One soul can help the whole world. You say, 'I want to do some work. Use me, here I am!' But, my child, you don't need to come to us to offer yourself. The service is here beside you, and waiting in your own heart every day. The greatest service that anyone can give is continually to think aright—continually to send forth love, to forgive.

Don't be in a hurry about spiritual matters. Go step by step, and be very sure. When the time is ripe, the opportunity will be given to you to do work which the Master has planned for you.

FLOWERS OPEN SLOWLY

Train yourselves to catch a vision of the Master over the heads of the throng, to hear his voice in your heart, guiding you gently to do those things which you have to do with courage and with peace. Then, my brother, you will not be without joy or hope. If things do not happen as you want them to happen, know that a better way is being found. Trust, and never forget that the true way is the way of love. Flowers do not force their way with great strife. Flowers open to perfection slowly in the sun.

. . . IS WISE IN SPEECH AND ACTION

WISDOM COMES

Wisdom comes to those who are calm and tranquil in spirit, to those who wait upon the Lord. Through an ever-increasing love in the heart you will grow wise.

THE WELL-SPRING OF TRUTH

Your spirit is part of God, and all knowledge lies within you. If, in your meditation, you will go deep within, you will find the centre of truth and of the infinite powers which await man's use. You will touch the spring of all happiness and health.

INTUITION

The way to truth is through the spirit. In the outer world is turmoil and chaos and unhappiness. You *think* with the mortal mind, with the mind which is part of the substance of earth. You should think with your inner mind; you should approach problems through the inner self, through intuition. The very word explains itself. In-tuition—training inside yourself. You are looking outside for help, and all the time the help you want is inside. The world of spirit that so many of you talk about and believe in, and long to touch, is all within.

SEE GOOD

In your search for truth, you must continually project thoughts of goodwill, brotherhood and love. Always see good, even if the good appears infinitesimal in comparison with other things. Let your thoughts of love and goodwill be broadcast. You cannot know how much good you will do, by allowing your higher mind to dominate your life.

BE UNDISMAYED

Work with the Light always, knowing that when you send out the Light you are helping to awaken and quicken the Light in all your fellows. Don't look down or back, neither be dismayed by unworthy little things which would trouble and disturb your spirit. Look forward into the Light, knowing that God is working His purpose out and all things work together for good for the man who loves God.

TO FIND A SOLUTION

The divine Mind ever seeks the good of the whole. Therefore, in all your earthly problems, seek not for the purely personal solution, but for underlying principles. If you can lay your problem beside a principle; or, in other words, if you can lay it beside the Master's thought, you will always find a true solution to it.

POWER OF THOUGHT

A disciple of the Master must gain a measure of control over his thoughts. We suggest that you start by taking yourselves in hand and asserting your mastership over the details of everyday life. Don't let your body do exactly what it wants, or your brain either. Assert your power of command over body and mind. This discipline will grow to be a habit.

PERSPECTIVE

If you want to get a clear picture of any condition in life, don't try to see things with your nose on them! See them from the highest point, from the plane of spirit, and you will be surprised at how different your problems look.

Resist pessimism and negative thinking both in private and national life. Think only good. 'Think God.' Whatever your trouble, put God, and thoughts of God, in place of that trouble. Think godly things. Even if he does not appear to be doing so, see that your brother man is striving towards God. See the world developing and growing more spiritual.

DO YOUR BEST

Do your best, even if you make apparent mistakes—how are *you* to judge if they are mistakes? You can only obey the higher urge which inclines you to contribute the best that you have to the service of the community of men and angels. Thus you shall be an ever-growing channel for the Light of the Master.

WHEN IN DOUBT, DO NOTHING

When you are in doubt, be still, and wait. When doubt no longer exists for you, then go forward with courage. So long as mists envelop you, be still; be still until the sunlight pours through and dispels the mists—as it surely will. Then act with courage.

YOU MAY NOT ALWAYS CHOOSE

You may not always choose your path. You stand before your Master awaiting his orders. But sometimes you are impatient; you demand and you expect instant action, instead of trusting your Heavenly Father and His ministers; trusting those into whose charge He has given you to help you, to guide you and guard you in all your ways.

BE STILL

Have confidence in that divine Love which holds you close. You have nothing to fear, and if you don't know which way to go, stay where you are. Just be still and quiet and you will find how remarkably conditions will work out for you. So much tangle is made by this eagerness to get on with something. You only get into a muddle and then have to retrace your steps. Be still and trust in God.

WAIT FOR GUIDANCE

Everything happens at the right moment, the acceptable time of the Lord. You on earth do not always know what that time is, but if you will follow the guidance of the spirit, waiting patiently for a clear indication for action, then you will be guided aright.

Instead of demanding your own way, be prepared to yield in humility and say: 'Dear Lord, show me *Thy* way; I trust in Thee. Lead me according to Thy will, for Thou alone art wise, Thy love is beyond my worldly understanding.' Then your way will be made plain.

GOD CAN SOLVE PROBLEMS

Sometimes you come up against a problem that seems quite insoluble by the mind or indeed by any material means. On such occasions surrender in true humility to the Great White Spirit. Give yourself into the hands of the Spirit; know that where man fails the power of God will never falter.

THE VICTOR

Man is spirit—this is all man needs to know;
and spirit is triumphant over matter.

THROW OFF YOUR CHAINS

The Great White Spirit, the Golden One, the
Source of all life, will not fail to raise you up
if you will allow yourselves to be raised. You
keep yourself in bondage, in chains! Throw
off the chains of this earthly darkness and see
yourself as you truly are, a son-daughter of the
blazing, golden Light of the Sun.

RISE INTO THE SUN

However difficult your pathway is, my child, daily seek the glory of the God-life. Soar, in your higher mind, in what the world calls your imagination; rise into the glorious Light of the spiritual Sun and know that this Light is the re-creative force which will flow through you, causing every ill to fade out of your body, and crooked places to be made straight.

CHRIST IS KING

You are a bearer of the Light, for you are as the Divine Mother, bearing within you the Light of the Son. Take this Light out into the world to bless and to heal, and quicken the vibrations of the whole earth.

YOUR GREATER SELF

When the will to become Christlike grows strong in the heart, it causes an opening in the consciousness for the greater self to descend into the physical body. You think that your physical body is you, but it is only an infinitesimal part of you. If you would contact your true self, go into a place of quiet to commune with your Creator in your heart. Then you will rise in consciousness. That great light to which you rise, is, you will find, the divine man—you, yourself, your own divinity, the real you. By opening your consciousness to this divine self your whole vibrations will be quickened and your body become purified.

THE MAGIC PRESENCE

The Christ within you is King . . . every particle, every cell of your body, is subject to the divine power and glory. Realise the divine magical presence within you. The Light overcomes all darkness.

LOOK TO THE STAR

When you are in the shadows, or you feel that the shadows are near, remember to look up, to visualise the blazing Star above you in the spirit spheres, and to feel its strength, its steadiness, its radiance, pouring into your heart. Go forward in confidence and in full consciousness of the light of this Star shining upon you.

WALK IN THE WORLD AS A CHILD OF THE LIGHT

You are spirit, you are immortal, you are a radiant being, a child of God! Live in your spirit and allow nothing to bind or limit you.

ABOVE THE CLOUDS

It is easy to be cheerful when there is everything to be cheerful about, but not so easy when the earth is shrouded in darkness—at these times your test comes. It is easy to be kind when everyone is kind, easy to be loving when others are loving. But in this there is little credit. The wise brother knows the Light is shining in the heavens even when the shadows are dense. Thus when you raise your consciousness above the clouds, you will know that the sun is shining and that the life of Christ is the only enduring life.

MEN LOOK TO YOU

Do not be beguiled by the attractions of materialism, or by the sorrows and anxieties which your karma brings. Have courage, for so many depend on you, your thoughts, your attitude; men are looking to you and unconsciously recognise in you a Light. They know that you have something which is helpful and good. Keep the Light shining in your heart and mind, and remember the great privilege which has been given to you to help lead man onward and upward to the glorious Morning Star.

What do we mean by sending forth the Light? Give out the love which you feel in your heart, and it goes forth as a Light. If you could see yourselves when you are truly sending forth the Light, you would see a great radiance flowing from your heart—from your head in many cases. Your aura would be shining. You would see the rays penetrating to a limitless degree; you would see the Light flowing from you, touching the heart, the understanding, even the physical life of your fellow men.

THE WHOLE ARMOUR OF GOD

When you earnestly send out the thought of love and light, you surround yourself with light—as you give you receive. The light which you send forth from your heart not only dispels the material and erroneous thoughts of others; it also creates a protective shield around you. This is what is meant by the words, 'Put on the whole armour of God.'

GOD IS MERCIFUL

The karma of the individual can be transmuted by the power of the Christ Spirit. We so frequently hear the thought: 'Oh, it is my karma, I must accept it.' It is true that you must accept divine law, but divine law is merciful, and the love of the Christ growing in your heart can release your soul from bondage.

HEALING FROM THE SUN

Basically all healing is the intake into the body of the eternal Sun, the Light. If you can call upon this Light, breathe it in, live consciously in this Light, it will actually control the cells of the physical body. The body is so heavy, material life so strong, that you forget the power of God to re-create tissue, to re-create the living cells of your body.

As a servant of the Christ you must never lack courage. It is a temptation to do so, for the shadows group around you and tempt you to be weary, to have no confidence; they tempt you to say, 'I am no use,' and to have what you call an inferiority complex. Never doubt the power of God to work through you. To think you are no good is to doubt God's power.

SEE THE BEST

Do not despair; do not dwell on the negative side of any situation, for you will do no good by this. Always put into operation the forces of construction. Believe that good will come, that the best is coming, and it will. We shall never forsake you. We also are God's children and His agents. We shall never forsake you, dear brother.

74

Relax mind and body and breathe slowly and deeply. As you breathe in, try to imagine that you are filling every particle of your being with God, with God's breath. As this love fills your heart and mind, every atom, every cell of your body will be filled with perfect life.

THE ONLY REALITY

Now be happy, be filled with joy and look forward into the Light. Live and move in that golden eternal Light, and know that nothing can hurt you. The only reality is the Light, is God, is Love.

... BEARS NO RESENTMENT

BLESSED ARE THE MEEK

Trust in God and have faith. If you know you have been rebellious, ask humbly for forgiveness, and then be kind and loving. Remember that this is man's only freewill choice —not whether he shall go this way or that way, but whether he shall on the one hand accept his experiences with true love and humility, or whether he will be rebellious and angry, and full of tortuous emotion. Seek to grow to Christ-manhood.

THE WAY TO TRANSMUTE KARMA

We come to you to help you. A thought from you, a prayer, a hope, and your brethren know and are with you; but we cannot take from you your freewill, nor rob you of your experience; we cannot free you from your karmic debts. You must accept for payment debts that you have incurred, and sweetly surrender yourselves to the infinite love of God. But we can assure you that your karma can be softened by the love of the Lord Christ. You can work out your lessons joyfully. This is the way to transmute karma. As soon as you have learnt the lesson your karma is meant to teach you, it will fall away; it will no longer exist.

IN TIMES OF STRESS AND DIFFICULTY

May it comfort you in times of stress and difficulty to know that all you suffer and endure, all the self-discipline that you go through is so worthwhile; it is not in vain, for it is carrying you forward and upward to the glorious, happy, perfect life. Keep bravely, courageously and hopefully on with your life, knowing that you are placed in the position that you hold through your past karma. Your present opportunities ought to be accepted gratefully. Always wait upon God, and the way will be shown to you, within yourself. We are with you, watching over you. We are all one Brotherhood, all in one and one in all.

BE PATIENT, HAVE FAITH

We know, beloved child, the sorrows and the difficulties of the material life lived in a physical body at present unawakened to the beauty of God's worlds. We know how hard it is to pursue the shadowed path. You have to walk in darkness, to accept the conditions in which you find yourselves, trusting in the love of the Great White Spirit. This is not easy, we know, but have patience and faith. Never doubt that all works together for good; never doubt the power, the wisdom and the love of God.

You do not need to attempt to stand up for your 'rights.' Realise that God adjusts things with exact law, and peace will return to your heart. Don't get fussed when things are difficult—be still.

ACCEPT, WITH LOVE

We advise you to love not only your fellow man, but also the conditions of your life. Bear no resentment. Nothing happens out of order or by chance, and the great Law brings those very conditions in your life which you need for growth. So accept with love all that happens. Look for the lesson that has to be learnt from the experience. Look up to God daily, hourly, and be filled with the divine light and love. It pours like a golden ray into the heart and head centre, cleansing, healing, uplifting, steadying, giving you control.

There is so much which you cannot understand in human relationship; often you have to endure what seems to be injustice. But those in the spirit world, who can take the long view, can always tell you that all crooked places will be made straight and all injustice will be righted.

GOD'S APPOINTMENTS

Do not be discouraged. Learn not to be disappointed in anything, or any person. You are disappointed because your will, your desire, has been frustrated. Learn to submit to the Divine Will, for His Will is all-wise. Wait, then, for *His* appointments, learning to tread the path wisely, serenely.

ACCEPTANCE

It is natural for the lower self to resent pain and suffering; but when you can surrender to

God, so that your heart overflows with love and acceptance of the wisdom of God's plan, then you can make real progress, and you are filled with a deep peace which it is beyond the power of the world to give.

GOD NEVER FAILS

God never fails His children. Do not seek for things to work according to your desires; or for your circumstances to be arranged according to your earthly will. But have faith that God is leading you on the path to ultimate happiness.

WHEN YOU ARE READY

Learn to bow to the will of God, remembering that there is an acceptable time of the Lord. God is infinitely wiser than His children, and His plan is perfect; His purpose for your life is spiritual growth and spiritual unfoldment. When you are ready, that which is prepared will be placed before you.

Be still, my brother, be still and wait for the pointer to point your way. You cannot make a mistake if you do this, but it could be catastrophic if you rushed forward because you would certainly come up against a sharp instrument which would be painful. This is the cause of man's suffering. Until he learns to wait patiently on the Lord he will suffer.

GOD WILL BRING SOMETHING MORE BEAUTIFUL

If you are called on to give up certain things; if God takes these things away, you have to learn resignation to His great love; to be at peace within, knowing that God will bring something more beautiful into your life.

THY WILL, O LORD

God holds the plan, my dear one, always God holds the plan, so when things do not go according to your plan, remember, do not fuss, just fit in. This doesn't mean letting go your responsibilities. It means that when you have done all you can according to your power, the rest is in God's hands. Take your mortal hands off, and let God work His will.

PRAYER

Usually people only pray for what they want, something for themselves. 'O dear God, give, give, give! Give me health, give me happiness, give me the necessities, give me all I want, dear God, and I will do what you want,' instead of saying, 'Dear Father, beloved Christ, I give myself to Thee; do with me as Thou wilt.'

WELL DONE, LITTLE BROTHER . . .

Pain and suffering so often come because you cling to a condition which obviously must be withdrawn. But once you have shown yourself willing to renounce, you will receive fresh

opportunities and greater blessing. We might
say that the Master's hand is then laid upon the
head of the pupil with the words, 'Well done,
little brother . . .'

REJOICE IN YOUR KARMA

Karma, my child, is really unlearned lessons.
These lessons have to be faced in a calm spirit.
Rejoice in your karma. Thank God for the
opportunities which are presented to you to
learn lessons and dispose of your karma, for
these are steps by which you mount into the
Great White Lodge.

YOU LONG FOR THE LIGHT

You pray earnestly for your problems to be
removed; you long for the light and for won-
derful spiritual ecstasy. But can you not see
that it is only by going through the discipline
of these outer things that your eyes are opened
and your sensitivity to heavenly truth in-

creased? You cannot taste and see until you have passed through this process of discipline. Therefore thank God for the trials and heartaches, which are disciplining your soul until it becomes able to comprehend and absorb the beauty of the heavenly life.

RENUNCIATION

The soul growing strong, the soul in whom the flame burns brightly, will face all renunciation philosophically, tranquilly, joyously. For that wise soul knows that what is lost has served its purpose, and something better now awaits the soul, though whether on the spiritual or the material plane it cannot know. Learn to face the cross with tranquillity, knowing that out of the ashes of the past new life is born.

... IS PATIENT, TRUSTING IN GOD'S GOODNESS AND HIS PERFECT PLAN

BE READY

Be ready at all times to accept the will of God, to accept the way which is put before you. Knowing there is no other, then meekly follow that path and trust in the great and glorious Spirit.

RESIGN THE REST TO GOD

The Law works without fail; therefore having done your best, resign the rest to God's mercy, wisdom and love. Never think that *you* know what is good for you. God alone knows, and He sends according to your need. Be humble, be patient, and trust!

LEAVE THE OUTWORKING TO GOD

Think of life as a vast whole. It is impossible for you to comprehend infinity, but this simple fact you can understand: a prayer, a thought, an aspiration to those in the heaven world, is never lost. Instantly you make that contact by prayer, or meditation, angels gather to help you to fulfil your aspiration and to answer a true prayer. It may not always be answered in the way *you* want, but it will be answered in a very much better way if only you will be content to leave the outworking of your prayer to God and His angels.

THE ACCEPTABLE TIME OF THE LORD

Everything happens at the *right* moment, the acceptable time of the Lord. You on earth do not always know what that time is, but if you will follow the guidance of the spirit, waiting patiently for a clear indication for action, then you will be guided aright.

LIVE TRANQUILLY IN GOD

Patience really means confidence in God, knowing that God has you in His care. God, the Great White Spirit, is all around you and in you and is working out a wise and beautiful purpose in your soul. Do not live with the feeling that you must get over the ground as quickly as possible to reach a certain point. Just live every moment, every hour, every day, tranquilly in the protective love of God, taking the hours as they come and doing one thing at a time, quietly.

NEVER DOUBT

Just surrender, and love God with all your heart and with all your soul and with all your mind; never doubt His wisdom. Then miracles will happen not only in your physical body but in your life and in your work.

All is a question of submission and surrender, of taking life steadily, tranquilly. This does not mean lack of effort, but effort of the right kind, continual effort to let the Christ Light take possession of your emotions, of your thinking, and of your actions. It means standing on one side and saying, 'Only God is great. I am nothing. All the good which has been accomplished in my life is the work of God.'

ALL IS GOOD

Know beyond all doubt that God is Love, and that all things work together for good for the man who loves God. See divine law operating in your own life and in the life of the whole of humanity. Look always for the good, look for God, and you will find that God's great love is working out a wise and beautiful purpose through human evolution.

Behind every dark happening, behind every difficulty, there is a hidden blessing. Man has to develop faith and confidence in God, knowing that at the right moment, at the acceptable time of the Lord, the magic will be worked, the dark shroud will fall away, and the radiant angel will be waiting. Behind all is the glory of God's life—the divine magic which illumines all life's happenings.

FOLLOW THE LIGHT IN YOUR HEART

Don't think that we are unaware of your disappointments and hardships, and the fears that possess you. We in spirit know that you have tests. We know that the physical body is not always as fit and perfect as it could be. We know that the material conditions in your life can be irksome. We are so attuned to you, our brother, that we absorb your feelings. We know the problems and the difficulties; but we would reassure every one of you that if you will truly follow the light within your heart, all will be well.

JUST LAUGH!

If everything goes wrong, just laugh! Just let it have its fling, let it go; but keep your vision upon God, and know that all will come right. All *will* come right—that is the truth!

NOT A SPARROW FALLS

Are you afraid of poverty, of lacking the necessities of life? Who feeds you and clothes you, my brother, my sister? None other than the Great White Spirit; He will never fail you if only you will attune yourselves to His life, surrender to His love and His wisdom; for He knows your needs, and will never fail in His supply. Only you cut yourselves off from this supply by forgetting that He is the Source of all, on every plane of your being, spiritual, mental, physical.

Things do not always work out as you pre-conceive them, but you must hold in your heart the knowledge that God's way is the right way. All things work together for good for the man who loves God. They must do, because he puts himself *en rapport* with God and then everything is good.

SEEK FIRST THE KINGDOM

Have no fear or anxiety; surrender your life and affairs into the hands of the Great White Spirit. Seek first the Kingdom of Heaven; seek the communion table and be strengthened in your heart for what lies before you. If you trust in God, His love will flow through your whole being, and all the affairs of your life, and you will know peace of heart.

GOD'S WISDOM

It is easy, on looking back, when you know how things have worked out, for you to say, 'How could I doubt?' But it is *now*, while the working out is in process, that you have to give your confidence to the divine Wisdom guiding your life. When you have experienced, when you have tasted the fruits spread on the heavenly table, you will see that nothing could have been altered. If you had your will, you would create great confusion and suffering for yourself, but God in His compassion protects you.

BE BEARERS OF JOY

My child, do not permit yourself to be pessimistic. You are bearers of joy and you must not be cast down or dismal about the world; the evolution of the race is steadily going forward and you must always see the progress, see the beauty, see the good outworking.

We know and understand the sorrows and troubles of your mortal life. And, because we understand, we ask you to strive to surrender your will and desires to the will of God, knowing that nothing happens by chance in human life, all the events follow a definite spiritual law. It is because you cannot see far enough along the road your spirit must travel that you become overwrought with fear and anxiety. God knows your need, and His angel servers are always active on the earth plane to bless and uplift humanity. All they need is the co-operation of human love.

NEVER FEAR

Never fear your journey ahead, for as God has watched over you all your life and, in spite of your fears, has brought you through all the trials and sorrows of your life, so He will take you through the darkest vale, into the light.

THE OUTCOME

We can speak so confidently about the outcome of all your human problems because we know that all human life is governed by a divine law, perfect in its outworking. The purpose of that law is to draw all men and women, all the human family, into a consciousness of God. Do not look backwards unless it is to say, 'How beautiful is the path that I have traversed!' Do not regret the past. You are moving forward, travelling life's path to find happiness once again, and this time an enhanced happiness.

BE THANKFUL

Concentrate your heart and life upon the Christ life and glory, and you will no longer fear anything. Be thankful, for thankfulness also casts out all fear. Be thankful, and remember that your Father in heaven knows your needs and all you need will be supplied.

Happiness is the realisation of God in the heart. Happiness is the result of praise and thanksgiving, of faith, of acceptance; a quiet, tranquil realisation of the love of God. This brings to the soul perfect and indescribable happiness. God is happiness.